A REBEL'S LIFE

NANDIKA SRIVASTAVA

INDIA • SINGAPORE • MALAYSIA

Contents

"Appreciation"

"Teenagehood"

A Rebel's Life

Yeah, we don't fit in,
but that's not a sin.
We are the villains of society,
but what about the thing they give us called anxiety?
This is a rebel's life,
We gotta strive to survive.

Our life is quite hard.
Rejection is always on our cards.
We aren't bad,
just a bit passionate and mad.
This is a rebel's life,
We gotta strive to survive.

They try to bully us out,
but they can't stop our shouts.
Everyone is against us,
don't we deserve a little trust?
This is a rebel's life,
We gotta strive to survive.

We can't afford to look down.
We always have to carry our crowns.

But we're like phoenix; we'll rise from the ash again,
I promise all your efforts will go in vain.
This is a rebel's life,
We gotta strive to survive.

Nerd

Yes, I'm a nerd.
But, on the basis that you call me a nerd, is absurd.
So what if I'm shy and quiet?
How on earth does that prove that I'm not right?
I feel suffocated when I'm with you guys.
I honestly think you're nothing but a bunch of hypocrites.

How come I am the villain when you shed your crocodile tears?
What if I'm really tired of your you-don't-belong-here stares?
I acknowledge that we don't have the same preferences or choices.
But does that make me so bad that you even get vexed by my voice?

I'm introverted, not stupid.
Remember, I'm no stranger to being secluded,
which means I don't need someone to rely on.
Be prepared, because I won't mind being the black swan.
I don't require attention to survive unlike you,
Your "fake" popularity seems trash in my view.

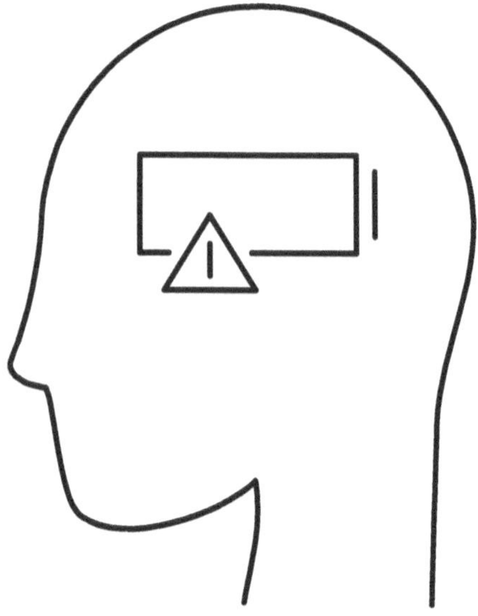

Why Do Life Sucks?

Why do life sucks?
Why is it all about luck?
Why can't a thing go my way?
Why those annoying people have a lot to say?

Why do I have to study without any will?
I'm young, and I want to chill.
Why do I have to follow that famous trend?
What's wrong with my messed up friend?

I don't see anything wrong in being rebellious.
Why do they accept everyone to be religious?
To all the adults who expect us to be "perfect"
We are objecting and we'll continue to object.
You cannot break our dreams,
just wait & watch, how we walk through your extremes.

14

Our Educational System

"Welcome to us"; we promise to give you a hard time.
Here, everything that isn't studying is a crime.
What? Few hours of studying is too less.
We apologize, but we couldn't be bothered about your stress.
Hobbies are forbidden under us.
Children take time, but they gradually adjusts.

I'll tell you a fact.
People were aware, but they didn't react.
We do discriminate between girls and boys.
We create a barrier and seize their joys.
We make girls wear long kurtas and boys a simple shirt,
so that those nasty girls don't dare seduce or flirt.
We disguise it in the name of culture.
This only applies to girls so that they don't become vulgars.

Poor are ignored and so is their potential.
Don't forget this information is confidential.
We even guarantee to ruin your child's mental health.
Sometimes, the child is even pushed to death.

We don't even assure your child a high paying job,
and that's how we succeed in our work to rob.
So please enroll your child in our "perfect" educational
system,
and then let them become our victims.

Insecurities

What actually is insecurity?
Well, it is something that general public regard as an
impurity.
Such as having too much body hair,
or having a complexion that isn't fair,
or having a big nose,
or wearing some non-trendy clothes.

But all this isn't limited to physical appearance,
It is also about belonging to a community treated with
indifference.
It is about not being social enough
Not being good in academic stuff,

Society demands us to be picture-perfect,
completely obedient and always correct.
And we corny humans just want to belong somewhere,
We require some love and some care,
So we give everything we are,
Just to learn are wishes aren't rare and nothing bizarre.

Well, insecurities might not be cool,
And those stares can be really cruel,
But I believe that the only disgusting thing in this world
are the standard who call us unwanted and ugly,
'Cause we are the one who decide, and every part of us is
beautiful and lovely
Let's not try so hard,
What is really beautiful is also odd.

One Day

Something is holding me back...
Or is it my lack?
Is this wrong or right?
Why am I stuck in this silent night?

What am I now?
Why is the world pulling me down?
Save me before the storm takes me away,
I'm scared, what if I fade away?

Why I am the only one here?
Is there someone who actually cares?
I'm tired of faking smiles...
and all the lies.
I don't deserve all these,
I can't lose everything please.

I'm locked up in a prison,
and all the hate has risen.
But one day I'll break free,
And find the long-forgotten real me.
One day, I'll end the reign of wrong,
And start my rule at the place where I actually belong.

One day, I'll be the one I was meant to be,
and just believe in the power 'we'
That one day will arrive soon,
as long as there is still the sun and the moon.

The Experience

No, I'm not interested in that thing,
so what I can't draw, dance or sing?
Am I not expected to stay happy the way I am?
I know my scores aren't that high in exams,
but why on earth I have to score that high?
I couldn't care less that I'm an introvert and shy.

I seriously don't want to do this or that.
I have no intention of running a race of rats.
Yes, I hate a lot of fools.
I accept I have broken some crazy rules.
I've always given my very best.
I was never the one who wanted to rest.

Alright, I confess I'm a rebel.
Yeah, I can't ride a bicycle with a pedal.
I know I'm a crybaby.
I know I'm not that model lady.
This fate was given to be for a reason.
I'm not eccentric; I just have a different vision.

I don't have a perfect life.
I'm still messed up inside.
I gotta learn a lot,
Give it my best shot.
And that's how we experience the "experience" though.
The first step is to accept your flaws and then glow.

I Just Feel Full of Frustration

I just feel full of frustration.
I am unable to get a hold of this situation.
The hostility present has become too much for me to ignore.
I can't pretend to be strong anymore.
My thoughts are overflowing with regret, failure, and sorrow.
I just want to lie down and forget about tomorrow.

I just feel full of frustration.
It hardly has any explanation.
I'm not depressed,
I'm only distressed.
It feels as though I'm running in circles endlessly.
A contributing factor can be jealousy.

I just feel full of frustration.
Perhaps I should try to engage in some conversation.
I'm longing for something I've never owned.
I can't help it. I'm already numb and cold.
The dream I dreamed seems impossible as time slips by.
And I can't do anything except cry.

I just feel full of frustration.
Everything seems merely an illustration.
I feel unimportant and useless.
There seems to be no end, and I'm clueless.
I can't really express my problems in lines.
I assume I can't really escape these dreadful times.

We'll See

The phrase that annoys me the most is "we'll see..."
Can't I just have the guarantee?
This phrase is the cause of most of the fights that takes place.
Because this is a neither 'yes' and nor 'no' case.
The phrase just hangs in there which leads to over thinking.
It might help postpone the decisions in the beginning.
But we know how horrible decisions are made in a hurry.
No matter what, they always lead us to worry.

But it's really easy and stress free to say this phrase.
You don't have to be anxious about the coming days.
So should I let myself loose or face the troubles?
Can anyone please help me with these struggles?

What We Were Taught Vs the Reality

They say that honesty is the best policy.

However, a child confronting an elder with the same candor isn't a good quality.

They say there is no substitute for hard work.

So why do wealthy achieve the success we deserve? Is it our bad luck?

"Your character will give you respect"

But when you're rich, your character doesn't matter, why though? I object.

"Be thankful to all things"

But what about those horrible ones which cannot be helped with pills?

"Unity is strength"

Politics, backstabbing, fights, where all these negative perks went?

Why the children are kept in a blur and left to discover the reality on their own?

This only result in their agony when they are grown.

'Cause whatever they thought is far different from the reality.

People are monsters, and this is just one of their brutalities.

Black Unicorn

I see myself as a black unicorn,
with a graceful body and a powerful alicorn.
It is mysterious and rare,
And definitely a dangerous enemy if you dare.
Not that innocent and pure typical unicorn,
but strong willed with magical horns.

Loyal if it gained trust,
fairy sprinklers or otherwise dust.
Hard to find,
but definitely one of a kind.

Why a 'black' unicorn, people wonder
Because black can be both the protector and hunter,
loves solitude and treasure weirdness,
and obviously, a big fan of fierceness.
Black is just like a bittersweet song,
and so is a unicorn.

Analytical and open-minded,
Others' opinions can't make it blinded.
Its life and will is immortal,

And its healing powers were never normal.
Never underestimate a black unicorn,
Believe me, disguised as a flower it is actually a prickling thorn.

Time and Uncertainty

The things I loathe the most,
are time and uncertainty.
It passes in a blink of eye,
And yet remains an eternity.

I sit by the window and ask the sky,
"Will I be able to embrace the future me?"
"Will I be contented when I'll die?"

But does that even matter?
I'm already a good friend of rejection and jealousy,
And yet I can't bring myself to start a new chapter.

How can I accept,
My roots would be alien to me someday
I guess, I gotta learn,
Everything won't be my way

No matter what,
I can't run away,
And I can't trust my gut.

They tell me to trust the procedure,
But I can't do anything,
I'm an over-thinking creature.

Take a Chill Pill

Chasing a wish is really hard,
and it truly sucks to be back at start.

Grasping the stars is impossible,
and the morning is unstoppable.

The time could be slipping from your hands,
the things won't always go according to your plans.

You can't embrace the sea,
You'll have to fail, dear me.

But take a chill-pill,
you're gonna reach that hill.

Give yourself a chance to breathe.
Let the sword again wear its sheath.

It's okay to take a break.
Sleep for a while in order to be awake.

Moonlight will guide you once again
One day, you won't have to feel that pain.

Get over it girl.
This ain't your ending but your birth.

"Life"

Bittersweet

Time is really bittersweet.
Few chords in life are kinda off-beat.
Both people and their memories leave gradually,
and we all gotta experience that individually.
However, it is what that helps us recognize our priorities,
But I still wish people could come with guarantees.

Mysteries are really bittersweet.
All of those questions will only repeat.
Aren't we too self-absorbed to think we're the only
inhabitants of universe?
Who knows, whether this is a blessing or a curse?
What will happen when we'll die?
Am I the only one stuck with all these 'whys'?

I guess our whole lives are really bittersweet.
There's just no way to cheat.
It is beautiful yet cruel.
We human evolve, but are still fools.

50

Cheers to Life

"Cheers to life"
The sins won't be washed away in afterlife.
We are the puppets of inevitability.
Our only saviors are our abilities.

"Cheers to life"
There is only misery and misfortune in sight,
but how does that even matter?
Sooner or later, the world's gonna shatter.

"Cheers to life"
The worst is yet to come by.
Humans are the worshippers of avarice,
and their end would be glamorous.

"Cheers to life"
It is a beautiful sacrifice.
There is no finish line,
just some memories, varying from the darkness to
cloud-nine.

Hate

We hate the mosquitoes not the butterflies,
We hate slow internet not the internet,
We hate some vegetables not all the meals,
We hate household work not cleanliness,
We hate bad experiences not the good ones,
We hate waking up in mornings not the mornings,

So why do we hate a whole group when only one member
has acted wrongly?
Who allowed us to hate on an entire nation for something
their leaders has done?
We'll give them hate and they'll give us hate
I don't understand, what comes as an outcome of this
cycle?
What does hating give us?
It will be either way,
We'll rather end the hate or it will end us
The choice is ours

Mirror of Truth

Once I found myself in front of the mirror of truth,
And god! His words were so cruel.

"Oh! the mirror of the truth,
tell me a truth about celebrities"
They go on pretending,
But there's no happy ending.

"Oh! the mirror of the truth,
tell me a truth about politicians"
They are the most annoying creatures of the world,
They'll only care, as long as the elections are concerned.

"Oh! the mirror of the truth,
tell me a truth about families"
Being born into a bunch of people doesn't make them
your family,
And expecting toxic people to change is insanity.

"Oh! the mirror of the truth,
tell me a truth about humans"
Most of them believe they are the "chosen ones"
And yet they only scare the one they are supposed to
protect with guns.

"Oh! the mirror of the truth,
 tell me a truth about life"
It is a beautiful torture,
Nobody can defeat it, even a warrior

"Oh! the mirror of the truth,
Tell me a truth about the truths"
A truth isn't supposed to be sweet,
A truth tells you where you are, in sky or in muddy streets.

New Beginnings

Dedicated to the new beginnings,
who are quite thrilling.
Like the waves of the sea,
which makes us together as 'we'

Despite all the problems and fights,
Hope is the thing which made it right.
To the memories left to recovered,
through the wound from which we just recovered.

These beginnings are like the clearance of fog,
And I believe that's what bought us all along.
Let us all thank the god to make us this strong.
and never go the way called wrong.

Two Types of Idiots

The first types are some vulgars.
They think they are different from others.
They are pretty disrespectful,
They think not, but their humor is dreadful.
They are narcissists, who are so full of themselves,
I wonder how can they consider themselves superior than
everybody else?
They badmouth their friends behind their back,
They want to be accepted and that's their lack.

The second one are those purest souls on this earth.
First of all, your act is absurd.
What's the point of pretending to be nice?
I bet this masquerade will cost a heavy price.
Do you think sacrificing makes you look cool?
Let me make this clear, you're nothing more than a fool.
You think this is how you were born?
Darling, you're completely and foolishly wrong
.

These were the two types of idiots,
They think their reality is too hideous.
Of course it is, but not as much as their fake personalities
Stop trying to fit in, and don't hide your bad qualities.

Awkward, Awkward

I guess, one thing everyone wanna escape are those awkward and embarrassing moments.
Such as an unreturned high five,
or saying good evening instead of good morning,
or when a friend leaves you with a friend of his,
or shouting in a public place unintentionally grabbing all the attention,
or burping loudly in a quiet place,
or accidentally mistaking a pedestrian as someone else,
or tripping in front of notables,
or leaving a shop without buying anything,

These are the worst types of circumstances.
But why do these unpleasant memories remain while the happier ones do not?

Aliens

I was always too fond of aliens and the other galaxies.
I was too eager to know about them and their families.
And I personally think they are much better than humans.
At least their so-called humanity isn't a delusion.

An alien isn't black or white.
An alien isn't body-shamed on the basis of his weight and
height.
An alien is neither poor nor rich,
and being mentally-disturbed isn't a glitch.
No alien is discriminated on the basis of religion.
and alien society can't interfere with an alien's decision.

I guess I was better off as an alien than a human being.
After all, a peaceful life with the aliens seems so much
appealing.

POVs

There are tears in her eyes because of him.

He doesn't wipe them because he fears he'll never be good enough for her.

She thinks of her forever companion and weeps while remembering their moments.

The friend of hers can't bring herself to say sorry because she feels like a burden.

He realizes that jealously and competition is ruining his sisters and his priceless bond.

So does the sister, but none try to clear the air in between.

She sniffs by the window and thinks that her parents don't love her.

On the other side, the parents are being harsh to her to make her ready for the world.

These are the point-of-views of people who lost their loved ones.

If desired, it is quite simple to restore all of these relations.

Talking the matter out can easily fix these fights that arise from nothing.

So, when you're in a fight, remember to consider their point-of-view and decide your actions.

Ego and Enemies

Having an ego is vital and yet a dangerous thing.
Most of us are terrible at dealing with the fights it brings.
People believe having an ego is rude and inconsiderate.
They refer to their ego as "self-respect", which is clearly different.

But, of course, our ego must remain under our control.
Otherwise, it turns us into as a monster as a whole.

It's just as necessary to have enemies as egos.
Enemies are the planters of the seed we can never grow.
They give the wisdom of knowing the difference between wrong and right,
and probably about learning to let go people who despise.

Both who and enemies are important for our growth as individuals.
Those who have too many egos and enemies are imbeciles.
The truth is, we're forever trapped with both of these things. And that's our reality.
Just accept that we ain't saints; It's just our destructive mentality.

It's Up to You

The first gift is of love and empathy.
The second gift is of hate and hostility.
The third gift is of fate and destiny.
The fourth gift is of endurance and stability.
The fifth gift is of intelligence and awareness.
The sixth gift is of creativity and insightfulness.
The seventh gift is of persistence and reliability.
The eighth gift is of capability and reliability.
The ninth gift is of passion and ambition.
The tenth gift is of stubbornness and curiosity.
Due to the fairness of god, some gifts are given in excess and others in less to every person.
Each gift carries the potential to be a disaster or a portal to other dimension.
It's up to you whether to call the gifts a curse or a blessing.

Wake Up, Stand Up and Fight

Locked up in your own illusion?
Can't find the solution?
Is it raining so heavily that you can't see things?
Not being able to spread those beautiful wings?

The tree of happiness is shedding its leaves.
Are you still looking for someone who understands your
needs?
Standing on the edge of life...
Trying and crying and dying...
But remember, a part of you is still alive.
Trying to survive...

Believe me, you'll also smile one day.
You will find the way.
Trust the god, he has given everyone a good life.
So wake up, stand up and fight.

A Journey to the Truth

Once I made up my mind to find the monster,
causing all the misery in the planet.
So I set out on a journey to save earth and it's inhabits.

I first encountered a scrawny boy with no arms.
"Oh my god, I promise I'll not leave that vile beast
without doing any harm"
I said to him while he just replied with a warm smile.
But it wasn't just warm, it was extremely hostile.
It craved revenge but was powerless,
but as usual, that feeble human laughed at all this mess.

Second, I met a woman with a swollen face.
She claimed that an acid attack,
had severely cost her grace.
I concluded that only that monster could have done this
cruelty.
But who on earth gave him the authority to ruin that
beauty?

I then ran into a girl near my age.
She was dressed as a bride and was probably attempting
to escape.
She saw me and stated, "They're really horrible"

I questioned her, "Was your marriage forcible?"
She chuckled,
"I was just one of the animals who escaped from being beheaded"
"And now loneliness is the only direction where I'm headed"
I really wanted to help her,
but there are some fights that you have to fight alone.
Frankly, nothing has changed and yet only my hunger increased to overthrew that monster from the throne.

I was running low on food when this weird looking man, dressed as a woman appeared before me.
He noticed me staring and said,
"Sometimes I just want to flee"
"Why?" I asked as he handed me some food.
"Because no matter what we transgenders are always refused"
"I'm sorry, but I really hope you can one day confide in yourself"
I got up and continued my journey due to the being's help.

And once again I blamed the monster for his sufferings.
But all these people kinda left me wondering,
and that was when I realized...

The monster that I was looking for was there all the time.

Humans are the one who ruined the things every time.

And the funny thing is that they claim that they side by peace.

But if that is true then why is the misery and misfortune in every street?

The Epiphany

Because there will never be a perfect globe.
I'm going to cope.
I'm still young, and my small queries don't matter.
It's me versus fate in this battle.

There is a lot of unfathomable concealment from us.
It is all left to be discussed.
My loved ones and those I despise aren't perfect; they
merely try their best.
I guess feelings were never meant to be expressed.

People come and go. It's in their nature.
Life's about finding our hidden treasures.
Our lives are too short to cry.
It's all about learning to rely.

The past won't recur, and the future cannot be foreseen.
The journey starts the moment you break yourself from
the routine.
Society doesn't matter and doesn't care about you.
What matters is whom you grow into.

"Appreciation"

Happenstance

Was it just a co-incidence?
How on earth did 'we' gained confidence?
Are you the wish that I've been waiting to come true?
or the stardust in the form of you?

I fall a little more for you as each day passes by.
It doesn't matter what I go through if you're my ally.

You're my firefly; even in this hopeless night you keep on
reminding me that there's still light.
I promise we'll go on holding hands throughout the days
and the nights.
We're still young and free.
There are still many dazzling nights we got to see.
The fate will have to surrender in front of us.
'Cause we are a syzygy formed due to trust.

Dreams

Our dreams aren't what we see in our sleep.
They are the one who makes us weep,
but we can't leave this thing like this.
It's a love we can't miss.

They tell us that it's impossible,
but even they admit our patience and hard work are
remarkable.
We wish to fly along with the clouds,
but only we worry and walk back and forth for hours.

"Will I ever be enough?" They wonder everyday.
"Will tomorrow be different from today?"
"They are a bunch of lunatics" people say behind us.
They say they don't see any potential in us.

We may have failed repeatedly.
We might be fools working relentlessly.
But does that means we'll give up?
Do they suppose us to depend upon our luck?

We swore to go on till the end.
We ain't the ones who'll pretend.
Our dreams can only ignite that fire in our hearts.
We do what we want, no matter the cost.

It's All Going to be Alright

I am aware of the difficulties we faced in the past few days.
We do, indeed, seem to be lost in a maze.
I think we can all reach the skies.
We just need to learn to try.
But believe me when I say,
We'll always continue the fight.
It's all gonna to be alright.

Let them criticize us.
Let us not underestimate the strength of us.
I promise we'll be doing fine.
We'll also shine.
Believe me when I say,
We'll always continue the fight.
It's all gonna be alright.

They won't manage to bully us anymore.
Even a lion would be afraid of our roars.
Don't let them change you.
I promise we'll get through.
Believe me when I say,
We'll always continue the fight.
It's all gonna be alright

It's Devastating How...

It's devastating how...
We are strangers now.
Well, I admit you're not the only one to blame.
I wish I hadn't turned a blind eye to your games.
I always pretended to be alright in front of you.
But I find it hard to imagine you with someone new.

It's devastating how
She's the one you adore now.
You act as if it is all my fault.
I failed to realize that this was your default.
I won't lie; she's far prettier and funnier than me.
I guess we weren't just meant to be.

It's devastating how...
I'm alone now.
I realize now that you've only come to me for favors.
It was stupid of me to ignore your behavior.
You said we would be forever,
Now why aren't we together?
Your memories become my nightmares every night.
As usual, I just shrugged it off by uttering "alright."

It's clearly devastating how...

No one is ever going to be by my side now.

I thought you wouldn't leave me when I was surrounded by some horrible beings.

However, you recently became one too and hurt my feelings.

But I'll make an effort to let go and go on like you.

Maybe someday I'll be happy too.

PINKY PROMISE

The Strongest One I Know

This one is dedicated to my loving sister,
First of all, you're an awful trickster.

You're the strongest one I know.
Even god can't describe our relation.
No matter what the situation,
You were that someone with no tears and fears.
Well, I hate to admit but you make my worries disappear.
I wish our relationship can remain like this all over the years.

But now the person who always smiles, is suffering from
a silent pain.
"Perfect" is the personality she is trying to maintain.
You don't need to prove your worth, at least not to me
I promise one day, the world will see

No matter what they tell you,
You'll always be the best at least, in my view.
I'll be never leave your side.
I wanna tell the world being pride.

MAX

The Problem with Farewells

I can't forget the last time when we came in for a hug together.
The last time we posed for a photo.
The last time we shared a laugh
The last time we ended up in tears together.
And it was probably the last time we ever met.

Having you was a blessing.
Having you was comfort.
Having you was the best part of the journey
Having you helped me to continue.
But leaving you is a disaster, and I can't do it.

I hate my feelings for you.
I hate my thoughts of you.
I hate the image of our time together.
And I really hate the sight of you leaving.

Why is it so difficult for me to face the reality?
Why can't I let go like others?
Why do things have to change?
I want to know, would we eventually become strangers?

The problem is in me, I know.

The problem is just I simply feel too much.

The problem is that sometimes, life demands some beautiful beings back.

The major problem is with farewells; we humans forget and move on in the end.

End of the Day

At the end of the day
I'm still at the same place
At the end of the day
I'm still wishing to rewrite the stars
At the end of the day
I couldn't befriend the odds

You never know
If we could go on forever
You never know
where the bright lights hide
You never know
If we could ever reach the magical jungle

It finally ended
And there's no looking back
It finally ended
But not my wishes and ambition
It finally ended
But some of those people never changed

This end is actually a new journey
And you've got no reason to be afraid
So this time, embrace the unknown
And get ready to dive in the sea of possibilities

The Unspoken

Show me your cuts.
I'll tell whether you got the guts.
Tell me your tale.
There is an answer to all your wails.
Let's run away from this tragic reality.
At this point, I prefer monsters than this humanity.

Don't be another bug who gets crushed by a foot.
Kill them as a poisonous bee would,
even though we won't ever meet again.
Our spring-like memories would always remain.

Destiny can't separate my love for you.
I can give up everything if I have to.
Speak the unspoken.
It won't matter if I'm broken.
I will fight the world if I get to meet you again.
Wait for me til' then.

Music

Music is my comfort zone,
because it was there when I felt alone.
Music is actually no big deal.
But sometimes it just turns into the thing called ideal.
It is funny how that tune doesn't have a specified tongue
But still can combine many as one.

It gives an another level of peace which humans largely
fail to give.
And not only peace; but also many memories you get to
relive.
I believe music is made of emotions, and so do humans.
The only difference is that humans make problems and
music their solutions.

I assume that a person's taste in music is like the shadow
of his personality.
It portrays his beliefs and mentalities.
I also do believe that music heals humans.
It gets you back on track because it has feelings.

For You

I can't pretend to be fine.
How can I accept that you won't be mine?
I don't want to go away, I can't imagine myself alone.
I can really feel this pain to my bones.

Have our forever came to an end?
I won't be ever fine without you, friend.
I never knew I loved you so much.
This thing is really the worst.

Would we really grow apart?
Can't I just go back to the start?
I hate myself and this situation
I can't yet let go this relation.
But to all my friends wondering if I'll miss them and our bond.
I will always remember us after the end and beyond

Thanks for being there.
Thanks for your care.
But I'm leaving because I have to.
And this end will have to do.

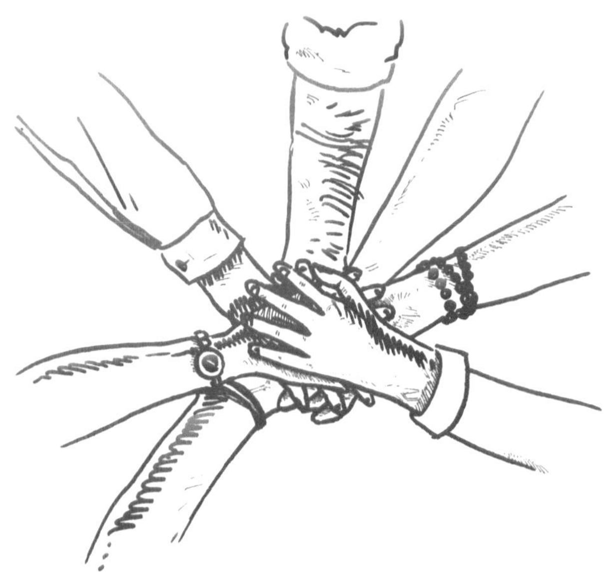

We

We laughed uncontrollably together.
We comforted each other in need.
We always made fun of each other.
We always had each other's backs.
We fought for delicious food.
We gossiped about people together.
We dreamed together, accompanied by dreamy clouds.
We walked holding each other's hands even when we were surrounded by negativity.
We just knew we were soulmates in the form of best friends.
We made playlists together.
We fought, but made up eventually.
We made memories that I'll continue to cherish until the day I die.
We complained about each other's stupidity.
But we had tears in our eyes at the thought of us separating.
I can say with certainty that you are the best thing that ever happened to me.
I'd like to thank you, my friend, for making me feel loved and accepting me the way I am.

Thank You

Thank you for cheering me up.
Thank you being someone I could count on.
Thank you for accepting my flaws.
Thank you for giving me a canvas to paint my dreams.
Thank you for fighting the world for me.
Thank you for being my father.

Thank you for trusting me.
Thank you for being a shoulder I could cry on.
Thank you for being worried about me.
Thank you for filling colors in my colorless life.
Thank you for never ever pressurizing me.
Thank you for being my mother.

I know I'm an ungrateful and stubborn brat to deal with.
I know I have never did things that would make you proud.
But I also know that I love you guys dearly.
I promise I'd try to be a better daughter.

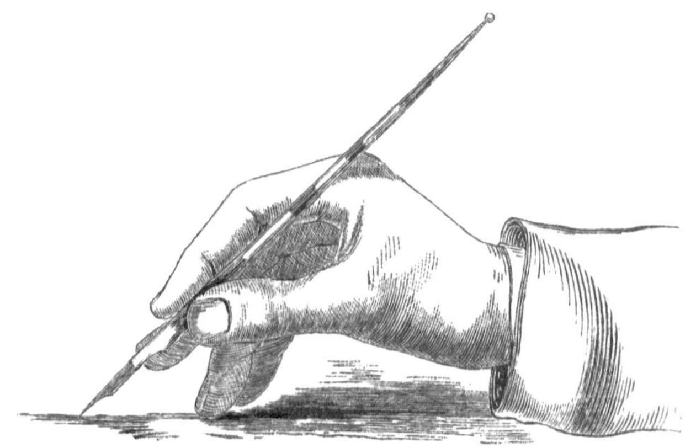

The Last One

It's funny how you made me love myself,
now that I look back at all bitter memories from the
disappointment shelf,
It feels good to have evolved from there.
You made me believe, there are people who care.

You said, it is never wrong to fight for the right,
Help yourself; throw the hesitation out of your sight.
I really appreciate finding you out of the blue,
The one who reshaped a loser is you.

To be honest, you can be really annoying at times,
It can be so hard to find the rhymes.
It is never perfect but still incredible,
and the satisfaction from weaving feelings into poetry is
inexpressible.

So this last one is dedicated to writing,
Thanks for coming into my life at the perfect timing.
I don't care if I don't earn money by doing you,
Doing you is doing me, and I know my feelings are true.
You are the paradise's key,
and definitely, the fate's call to me.

www.ingramcontent.com/pod-product-compliance
Lightning Source LLC
Chambersburg PA
CBHW062230150726
47991CB00006B/2509